SADLIER

PRAYER CELEBRATIONS FOR THE LITURGICAL YEAR

Thomas H. Morris

Consultants

Gerard F. Baumbach, Ed.D.

Eleanor Ann Brownell, D.Min.

Moya Gullage

William H. Sadlier, Inc.
9 Pine Street
New York, New York 10005–1002
http://www.sadlier.com

Nihil Obstat
✠ Most Reverend George O. Wirz
Censor Librorum

Imprimatur
✠ Most Reverend William H. Bullock
Bishop of Madison
September 23, 1997

The *Nihil Obstat* and *Imprimatur* are official declarations that a book or pamphlet is free of doctrinal or moral error. No implication is contained therein that those who have granted the *Nihil Obstat* and *Imprimatur* agree with the contents, opinions, or statements expressed.

Printed in the United States of America.

S® is a registered trademark of William H. Sadlier, Inc.

Home Office:
9 Pine Street
New York, NY 10005-1002

ISBN: 0-8215-5640-1
123456789/987

CONTENTS

USING THIS BOOK OF PRAYER CELEBRATIONS

his is a book of prayer celebrations for the various seasons of the liturgical year. You can use it with other members of your catechetical group and also with your family. Whenever we pray with other Catholics, Christ is present with us and the Holy Spirit guides our prayer.

❋ This is your prayer book. To make it truly your own, a shaded Response Box is provided where you can write some of your thoughts, prayers, and ideas for celebrating. Also, on pages 62–63, an outline is provided so that you and your groups can prepare your own prayer celebration focused on a theme, event, or need that is of particular concern in your lives.

❋ The prayer celebrations follow the liturgical calendar. Usually there is more than one celebration for the season. In most of the celebrations, you will have a choice of Scripture passages to read, and you will choose the songs to open and close the prayer service. This means that you will have a number of decisions to make as a group before the prayer celebration.

❋ Group preparation will be an important part of each and every prayer service. Before the celebration you will have the opportunity to read the Scriptures you will be using in the service. There are questions pertaining to the readings that will help you to reflect on the readings, your own needs, and the needs of the Church and the world.

❋ Before almost every prayer service, there are suggestions for symbols you can incorporate into the celebration that will help you focus on the message of the prayer service. The symbols suggested are all easy to find or make, but you may find that sometimes you will have better ideas. Symbols can help you to focus your minds and hearts on the word of God.

❋ Because the word of God is at the center of our prayer time, you will need your *Catholic Student Bible* for preparing the prayer service. You will probably want a second copy at home so that you can read and pray the Scriptures chosen for the prayer celebration.

❋ Setting aside a place for the prayer is important. Sometimes you may want to pray these celebrations in your parish church. Other times, you will choose a different place. Make sure ahead of time that the place where you would like to pray will be available for your use.

❋ Music is a very important part of prayer celebrations. Choose music that will help you to pray. The hymns and songs used at Mass will often tie into the themes of your seasonal celebrations, but listen closely to the lyrics of music from other sources as well. You may be surprised by what you will find when you begin to look for it!

❋ Another important part of liturgy is the prayer we offer for the needs of others. There are many opportunities for you to do this in these celebrations.

These prayer celebrations offer you many opportunities to pray together. May they lead to a deeper understanding of the prayer life of the Church expressed in the different seasons of the liturgical year.

WE PRAY WITH THE CHURCH

The center of our Catholic life is Jesus Christ. All that we do and pray and celebrate in the Church centers around him in a great seasonal cycle called the liturgical year. Within the cycle of a year, the Church unfolds for us the whole mystery of Christ. We enter into this mystery and follow Christ from his incarnation and birth through his passion, death, resurrection, and ascension to the day of Pentecost and the expectation of his return in glory.

The liturgical year begins with Advent, a time of joyful expectation, in which the Church voices our longing for the advent of the kingdom of God when Christ, who came among us at his incarnation, will come again in glory at the end of the world. To see the kingdom we need to move from the darkness of sin and doubt to the light of faith, the light of Christ. Christmas is the celebration of Christ, the Light of the World, the invisible God made visible.

The season of Lent follows—a time of preparation, a forty-day "retreat" before Baptism for new catechumens, and, for the rest of us, a time to renew and reaffirm what this sacrament means in our lives. Lent leads us to the Triduum, the "three days" in which we follow Christ from Holy Thursday, to his death on Good Friday, to his rising on Easter. The season of Easter lasts for fifty days.

Between Christmas and Lent and from the end of the Easter season until Advent is a period that the Church calls "Ordinary Time." This does not mean that these days are "just average" or "second-rate." Here *ordinary* means "not seasonal." We no longer pray according to the themes of Advent, Christmas, Lent, or Easter. Instead the Church concentrates on just one of the gospels. We hear not just the "big stories" but all the in-between stories of the parables, miracles, and teachings of Jesus. Ordinary Time reminds us that the kingdom is found in our everyday, ordinary efforts to grow in the image of Christ.

CELEBRATING THE SEASON OF ADVENT

Advent is the first season of the Church's year. It continues for four weeks and ends on Christmas Eve. The word *advent* means "coming." In the darkness of winter we joyously await the coming of Christ, the Light of the World.

The season of Advent urges us to prepare for the two comings of Christ: the first coming at his birth, and the second coming of Christ at the end of time. Advent is a season both of expectation and preparation. We wait in joyful expectation for the Lord's return in glory, and we prepare as a community to celebrate the birth of Christ.

Several customs and practices help us to celebrate this season of the Church's year. One such custom is the lighting of the Advent wreath. The Advent wreath helps us to mark the four weeks of our preparation. Each week, we light an additional candle on the Advent wreath. The light grows as we approach the celebration of the birth of the Light of the World, who shatters the darkness of sin and death.

One prayer we recite often during Advent is the Maranatha. It means "Come, Lord Jesus, come." We use this prayer in two ways: The first is to remember that our ancestors in faith awaited the coming of the promised Messiah. The second is that we now await the return of Jesus, our Messiah, in glory.

The liturgical color used during Advent is violet. It expresses our joyful waiting for Christ. As we remember his first coming at his birth, we turn our hearts and minds toward his second coming in glory.

BLESSING OF THE ADVENT WREATH

 ## Focus on Scripture
Readings: Isaiah 9:1–2; Luke 1:68–71, 78–79

Split up into two groups. Each group reads one of the passages from Scripture suggested for this prayer service.

God leads us to rejoicing in the reading from the Book of Isaiah, to peace in the Gospel of Saint Luke. The group that reads the passage from Isaiah should briefly answer the following question: When you are happy, how do you express your happiness? The group that reads from Luke should respond to the question: When you desire peace in your life, what is one thing that you do to achieve it? Share your thoughts.

Name one way you can express your joy or peace during the season of Advent.

Response Box

Enriching Your Celebration

Each person carries a short piece of evergreen that will be placed in a frame for the Advent wreath during the prayer. Join in a procession to enter the place where you will celebrate. Divide your prayer group into four sections. When you pray the Maranatha during the blessing over the wreath, say together four times, "Come, Lord Jesus, come." Each time you make this response, one of the groups will add its greenery to a section of wreath. The Advent wreath is completed when all the groups have contributed. Have one person from each group place the four Advent candles on the wreath (one for each week of Advent). Three candles should be purple, one rose-colored, symbolizing the joy of Christ's coming.

A fifth candle (a white one) should be lit before your prayer service and carried in your procession. Use it to light the Advent wreath candles. The white candle represents Jesus, the Light of the World. Just as it serves as the source of light for each candle on the wreath, so Jesus, the Light of the World, is the source of our joy and hope during this season of anticipation.

(Note: If fire laws do not permit lit candles, use battery-operated ones.)

PREPARATION

BLESSING OF THE ADVENT WREATH

The blessing of the Advent wreath usually takes place on the First Sunday of Advent.

Gathering Song

All come in procession singing and carrying greens for the wreath.

Greeting

All make the sign of the cross.

Leader: † In the name of the Father, and of the Son, and of the Holy Spirit.

All: Amen.

Leader: Let us bless the Lord.

All: Who made heaven and earth.

Leader: My friends,
as we begin this season of Advent,
we gather to bless this Advent wreath.
May it help us to prepare to welcome Christ
into our hearts and lives.

All: Amen.

Scripture

All sit during the reading of Scripture.

Reader: A reading from. . . .

The group chooses one of these readings:

■ Isaiah 9:1–2   ■ Luke 1:68–71, 78–79

At the end of the reading:

Reader: The word of the Lord.

All: Thanks be to God.

The Blessing of the Wreath

All stand around the Advent wreath.

Leader: Good and gracious God,
we eagerly await Christ's coming.

All: Come, Lord Jesus, come.

Leader: Let this wreath remind us
of Christ's unending love for us.

All: Come, Lord Jesus, come.

Leader: Let the candles remind us of Christ,
who is the Light of the World.

All: Come, Lord Jesus, come.

Leader: Let the green branches remind us
of our hope in Christ, our life.

All: Come, Lord Jesus, come.

All extend hands in blessing over the wreath.

Leader: Loving God,
we ask you to send your blessing
on this Advent wreath.
May its light remind us
of Christ's presence.
We pray this in the name of Jesus.

All: Amen.

The first candle is lit. An appropriate acclamation is sung.

Prayers of Intercession

Leader: My friends,
let us pray to God for our needs.

Reader: We pray for the Church,
that we might always walk
in the light of Christ.
We pray to the Lord.

All: Lord, hear our prayer.

Reader: We pray for the leaders of the Church:
our pope, our bishop, our pastor,
and all who lead us in the way of Jesus.
We pray to the Lord.

All: Lord, hear our prayer.

Reader: We pray for leaders of government,
that they act with justice and mercy.
We pray to the Lord.

All: Lord, hear our prayer.

Reader: We pray for all the sick
and those who care for them, especially:

(Name the sick you wish to pray for:)

We pray to the Lord.

All: Lord, hear our prayer.

Reader: We pray for those who have died,
and their families and friends, especially:

(Name those who have died you wish to pray for:)

We pray to the Lord.

All: Lord, hear our prayer.

Reader: And what else should we pray for?
(Those who wish add their petitions.)

All: Lord, hear our prayer.

Leader: Gracious God, we place these cares in your
hands, confident that you will give us the
gifts we need to be always faithful to you.
We pray this in the name of Jesus.

All: Amen.

Leader: Let us pray the words Jesus gave us.

All: Our Father. . . .

Closing Prayer

Leader: Loving God, we thank you for this day.
May we use this Advent wreath to remind us
always to follow Jesus our Lord.

All: Amen.

Leader: Let us bless the Lord.

All: And give God thanks!

Closing Song

PRAYER DURING ADVENT

Focus on Scripture

Reading: Isaiah 49:8–9, 11–13, 16

The Scripture reading for this prayer service comes from the Book of Isaiah. Take a few minutes to read the selected verses to yourself.

Do you feel that God has ever answered one of your prayers? If so, how has he answered you?

Share your responses with the other members of your prayer group before beginning the service.

Now together choose the intentions for which you wish to pray during this prayer service. Write them on page 12.

Enriching the Celebration

When bells are rung they call people to attention and signal a need to make an announcement. For this prayer service, you might want to use a bell. As a group, stand in a circle around your Advent wreath. Have a hand-held bell available for your use and have one person ring the bell as you say together, "Come, Lord Jesus, come."

As people of faith, you are sure of the coming of the Savior. The bell can serve as an announcement to God that you are prepared to follow the way of Christ in your daily lives.

PRAYER DURING ADVENT

Gathering Song

All stand.

Greeting

All make the sign of the cross.

Leader: † In the name of the Father, and of the Son, and of the Holy Spirit.

All: Amen.

Leader: Let us bless the Lord.

All: Who made heaven and earth.

Leader: My friends,
let us continue
to prepare the way of the Lord.

All: Come, Lord Jesus, come.

Lighting of the Advent Wreath

Week One: Light the first candle now.

Leader: You teach us to love God and one another.

All: Come, Lord Jesus, come.

Week Two: Light the second candle now.

Leader: You bring us God's mercy.

All: Come, Lord Jesus, come.

Week Three: Light the rose-colored candle now.

Leader: You bring us God's peace.

All: Come, Lord Jesus, come.

Week Four: Light the fourth candle now.

Leader: You come to set us free.

All: Come, Lord Jesus, come.

Scripture

All sit. Divide the group into two for the reading of the Scripture.

 Reader: A reading from the Book of Isaiah. *(Isaiah 49:8–9, 11–13, 16)*

Group 1: Thus says the LORD:
In a time of favor I answer you,
on the day of salvation I help you,
To restore the land
and allot the desolate heritages,

Group 2: Saying to the prisoners: Come out!
To those in darkness: Show yourselves!
Along the ways they shall find pasture,
on every bare height shall their
pastures be.

Group 1: I will cut a road through all my
mountains,
and make my highways level.

Group 2: See, some shall come from afar,
others from the north and west,
and some from the land of Syene.

Group 1: Sing out, O heavens, and rejoice, O earth,
break forth into song, you mountains.
For the LORD comforts his people
and shows mercy to his afflicted.

Group 2: See, upon the palms of my hands I have
written your name;
your walls are ever before me.

At the end of the reading:

Reader: The word of the Lord.

All: Thanks be to God.

Prayers of Intercession

Leader: My friends, let us pray to God for our needs.

*Write your own petitions for the Church, the world, and
your community:*

Reader: Loving God,
we turn to you
during these special days of waiting.
Keep our hearts open to your love.
We pray this in the name of Jesus.

All: Amen.

Leader: Let us pray the prayer Jesus taught us.

All: Our Father. . . .

Closing Prayer

Leader: Good and loving God,
increase our desire
for your presence in our lives,
and give us the strength we need
to grow in your love.
We pray this in the name of Jesus.

All: Amen.

Leader: Let us bless the Lord.

All: And give God thanks!

Closing Song

LATE ADVENT PRAYER

Focus on Scripture

Readings: Isaiah 11:1–3; Philippians 4:4–7

Choose either the reading from Isaiah or the reading from Philippians for your prayer service and read it once together before your celebration. Take a moment to answer one of the following questions.

If you are preparing the reading from Isaiah:

What is one additional name you would use to address the spirit of the Lord?

If you are preparing the reading from Philippians:

Is there someone, some place, or something that makes you feel close to God?

Share your responses with your group.

Now together choose the intentions for which your group wishes to pray in this celebration. Write them on page 15.

Enriching Your Celebration

Make a group banner. Find a large piece of purple or violet felt cloth. Cut out a photograph or draw an image of whatever makes you feel close to God. For example, if you feel closest to God when you are hiking in the mountains, cut out a photograph or make your own depiction of a mountain and attach it to your violet cloth.

When you see this banner, allow it to serve as a reminder of the people, places and things that make you and your friends feel close to God. Be sure to pray in thanksgiving for all those people and things when you are praying your petitions!

LATE ADVENT PRAYER

To be used during the final week of Advent (December 16–24).

Gathering Song

All stand.

Greeting

All make the sign of the cross.

Leader: † In the name of the Father, and of the Son, and of the Holy Spirit.

All: Amen.

Lighting of the Advent Wreath

The four candles are lit.

Leader: You come to set us free.

All: Come, Lord Jesus, come.

The O Antiphons

Group 1: O Wisdom of God,
guide us in the way of truth.

All: Come, Lord Jesus, come.

Group 2: O Holy Lord,
save us with your mighty love.

All: Come, Lord Jesus, come.

Group 2: O Flower of Jesse's Stem,
be a sign of love to us.

All: Come, Lord Jesus, come.

Group 2: O Key of David,
free us from the darkness.

All: Come, Lord Jesus, come.

Group 1: O Radiant Dawn,
shine on us to show us the way to you.

All: Come, Lord Jesus, come.

Group 2: O King of All Nations,
bring us together as one people.

All: Come, Lord Jesus, come.

All: O Emmanuel,
God's presence among us.
Come, Lord Jesus, come.

Scripture

All sit during the reading of Scripture.

Reader: A reading from. . . .

The group chooses one of the readings:

■ Isaiah 11:1–3   ■ Philippians 4:4–7

At the end of the reading:

Reader: The word of the Lord.

All: Thanks be to God.

Prayers of Intercession

All stand.

Leader: As these days of Advent come to an end,
let us turn to God and pray for our
needs and the needs of others.

*List the petitions of your group for the Church, the world,
and the community:*

All: Lord, hear our prayer.

Leader: Loving God,
hear the prayers of your children
gathered together.
May we always remember
the needs of others.
We ask this in the name of Jesus.

All: Amen

Leader: Let us pray the prayer Jesus gave us.

All: Our Father. . . .

Exchange of Peace

Leader: My friends,
we have kept watch together
as we wait for the final coming
of Jesus.

All: Come, Lord Jesus, come.

Leader: Now we are ready to celebrate
his first coming at Christmas.

All: Come, Lord Jesus, come.

Leader: The gift of Jesus to the world
is the source of our unity;
we were all made children of God
through the gift of his life.

All: Come, Lord Jesus, come.

Leader: My friends,
as a sign of that unity
and as a sign of the hope we share,
let us offer one another
a sign of peace.

All exchange the sign of peace.

Closing Prayer

Leader: Loving God,
we celebrate the new life you bring!

All: Rejoice in the Lord always!

Leader: Loving God,
we rejoice in these days of
preparation!

All: Rejoice in the Lord always!

Leader: Loving God,
We wait in hope for the final return
of Jesus!

All: Rejoice in the Lord always!

Leader: Father,
may the Christmas feast
we are prepared to celebrate
with family and friends
bring great joy to our hearts.
We pray this in the name of
Christ, your Son,
in the unity of the Holy Spirit.

All: Amen.

Leader: Let us bless the Lord.

All: And give God thanks!

Closing Song

CELEBRATING THE CHRISTMAS SEASON

he season of Christmas is the Church's joyful celebration of the mystery of the incarnation—Jesus Christ, the Son of God, became one of us:

> And the Word became flesh
> and made his dwelling among us. . . .
> John 1:14

Christmas is the feast of our salvation, for on this day, the Church tells us, "earth was joined to heaven."

The liturgies of the Christmas season, which extends from Christmas Eve to the feast of the Baptism of the Lord, are filled with images of light and hope. We pray with the Church in the Christmas Mass:

> Father,
> we are filled with the new light
> by the coming of your Word among us.
> May the light of faith
> shine in our words and actions.

This prevailing image of light is the origin of the custom of Christmas lights—on our trees, in our homes, in the Christmas cribs. Because of Christ's saving presence in our world, the darkness of sin and death is overcome and the Church is "filled with wonder at the nearness" of God.

One of the feasts of the Christmas season is the beautiful feast of Epiphany. On this day the Church celebrates the manifestation of the Savior to the world—represented by the three wise men who came from afar to find him and to offer him gifts. Again the image of light shines through the liturgy. The Church prays in the Mass for this feast:

> The wise men followed the star,
> and found Christ who is light from light.
> May you too find the Lord
> when your pilgrimage is ended.

The liturgical color for this season is white—a color that symbolizes the light and joy of this season.

BLESSING THE MANGER

 ## Focus on Scripture

Reading: Luke 2:1, 4–9, 11, 13–14

This is a prayer service you might want to celebrate at home. The text of the Scripture reading is printed in your book. Although this is probably one of the readings from Scripture you are most familiar with, take a minute to read it over quietly. Place yourself in the scene with Mary and Joseph as they travel to Bethlehem. Listen with the shepherds to the angel's message and follow them to the stable. Kneel before Jesus in wonder and joy.

Is there someone or something you, as a group, wish to pray for today? Write your intentions on page 20.

Enriching Your Celebration

Think of one important message you have heard in the reading from Luke's Gospel. Copy it onto a strip of paper. Each family member can contribute a message strip. Put these in a place where all can see them and be reminded of the gospel message.

BLESSING THE MANGER

The manger or nativity scene should not be displayed until Christmas Eve. The following celebration can be prayed at home.

Gathering Song

All stand.

Christmas carol:

Greeting

All make the sign of the cross.

Leader: † In the name of the Father, and of the Son, and of the Holy Spirit.

All: Amen.

Leader: How good it is for us to come together to remember and celebrate the birth of Christ who came so we could be free.

All: Rejoice in the Lord always!

Leader: Together, as a family, we will bless this Christmas scene. As we display it in our homes, it will remind us of God's gift of love to all the world. May we always live in that love!

All: Rejoice in the Lord always!

Scripture

(Luke 2:1,4–9, 10, 11, 13–14)

All sit during the reading of Scripture.

Leader: Let us listen together to the story of the birth of Jesus, so we can keep these words always in our hearts.

Reader 1: A reading from the Gospel of Luke. In those days a decree went out from Caesar Augustus that the whole world should be enrolled.

Reader 2: And Joseph too went up from Galilee from the town of Nazareth to Judea, to the city of David that is called Bethlehem, because he was of the house and family of David, to be enrolled with Mary, his betrothed, who was with child.

Reader 3: While they were there, the time came for her to have her child, and she gave birth to her firstborn son.

Reader 4: She wrapped him in swaddling clothes and laid him in a manger, because there was no room for them in the inn.

Reader 5: Now there were shepherds in that region living in the fields and keeping the night watch over their flock. The angel of the Lord appeared to them and the glory of the Lord shone around them, and they were struck with great fear.

Reader 6: The angel said to them, "Do not be afraid; for behold I proclaim to you good news of great joy. . . . For today in the city of David a savior has been born for you who is Messiah and Lord."

Reader 7: And suddenly there was a multitude of the heavenly host with the angel, praising God and saying:

All: "Glory to God in the highest and on earth peace to those on whom his favor rests."

Reader 1: The word of the Lord.

All: Thanks be to God.

As a response to the reading, the group can sing the refrain to "Angels We Have Heard on High."

Prayers of Intercession

Leader: Dear family [and friends], this feast of Christmas reminds us of God's great love for us. Let us turn to God now and remember those in need.

Share the petitions of your group or family:

Leader: Let us pray the prayer Jesus gave us.

All: Our Father. . . .

The Blessing of the Manger

Leader: Good and gracious God, you sent Jesus as your gift of love so that we could walk in your ways. Bless this manger and all who look at it. Let it remind us of Jesus and his call to us to follow him. We pray this in the name of Jesus.

All: Amen.

Leader: Let us celebrate the Christmas feast!

All: Thanks be to God!

A celebration of song with Christmas carols and Christmas treats can follow.

A FAMILY EPIPHANY CELEBRATION

 ### Focus on Scripture

Readings: Matthew 2:1–11; Psalm 24:1–2; 7–10

Tradition holds that the names of the three wise men, or magi, were Caspar, Melchior, and Balthasar. Following the star of Bethlehem, these wise men found the Holy Family and presented the infant Jesus with gifts. If the wise men were to come to your house, what spiritual gifts would you like them to bring to your family? Would you like them to bring peace or patience or joy or . . . ?

What are three spiritual gifts you think your family would like to receive?

Is there anything you can do as a family to give one another the gifts you long for?

Enriching Your Celebration

Attach a star to a stick to be carried by a family member. Use incense, perfumed lotion, and a golden ornament to represent the gifts of the wise men. Have members of your family carry these gifts as you move through your house in procession following the star. Before the closing prayer, go to the place where you display your manger and place the gifts beside it.

Allow the gifts of the wise men to remind you of the gifts your family truly needs.

Many Catholics traditionally have their homes blessed on the feast of the Epiphany. The following celebration can be prayed at home. You will need chalk and holy water (which you can bring home from your parish). All of the family should come together for this special blessing. You can also invite neighbors and friends.

Gathering Song

Stand.

Greeting

All make the sign of the cross.

Leader: † In the name of the Father, and of the Son, and of the Holy Spirit.

All: Amen.

Leader: Let us give thanks and praise to God for making his dwelling with us.

All: Rejoice in the Lord always!

Leader: Let us give thanks and praise to God who fills our home with peace.

All: Rejoice in the Lord always!

Leader: Let us give thanks and praise to God. May all who enter this home find the welcome and love of Christ.

All: Rejoice in the Lord always!

Scripture

All sit. Form two groups for a reading of Psalm 24:1–2, 7–10.

Group 1: The earth is the LORD's and all it holds,
the world and those who live there.

Group 2: For God founded it on the seas, established it over the rivers.

Group 1: Lift up your heads, O gates; rise up, you ancient portals, that the king of glory may enter.

Group 2: Who is this king of glory? The LORD, a mighty warrior, the LORD, mighty in battle.

Group 1: Lift up your heads, O gates; rise up, you ancient portals, that the king of glory may enter.

Group 2: Who is this king of glory? The LORD of hosts is the king of glory.

All: Glory to the Father, and to the Son, and to the Holy Spirit.
As it was in the beginning, is now, and will be for ever. Amen.

The Blessing of the Home

All stand.

Leader: Good and gracious God, you led all nations to Jesus by the star in the sky. In Jesus, we find our new home. Bless this house, all who live here, and all who visit here. May we live in Christ's light and bring that light to others.
We pray this in the name of Jesus.

All: Amen.

Procession to the Doorway

Leader: The front doorway of this home
is the symbol of welcome.
There we greet all in the name of Christ.
Let us go together to that place
so we can bless it.

Procession Song

While going in procession to the front door, a song can be sung.

Leader: *Holding the holy water.*
This holy water reminds us of our
baptism. We welcome all as Christ.

The holy water is sprinkled on the doorway.

We remember those travelers
who were welcomed by the Holy Family:
Caspar, Melchior, and Balthasar.
We mark this doorway
with their initials
and the date of this new year.

*The following symbols are written on the door
or doorpost in chalk: †C †M †B. The first two
digits of the current year are written before the
initials and the last two digits after the initials.*

May God bless and protect
all who pass through this doorway.
We pray this in the name of Jesus.

All: Amen.

All return back inside the house.

Exchange of Peace

Leader: Dear family [and friends],
God has blessed our home with his love
and the love we share.

All: Rejoice in the Lord always!

Leader: In this home, we pray that
all will feel the welcome of Jesus.

All: Rejoice in the Lord always!

Leader: In this home, we pray that
we will be safe from all harm.

All: Rejoice in the Lord always!

Leader: As a sign of the unity and love we share,
let us offer each other a sign of peace.

All exchange the sign of peace.

Leader: Let us pray the words Jesus gave us.

All: Our Father. . . .

Closing Prayer

Leader: May Christ always find
a dwelling place of faith
in our hearts and in our homes.

All: Amen.

Leader: Let us bless the Lord.

All: And give God thanks!

Closing Song

Celebrating the Season of Lent

The season of Lent is a time of preparation for the celebration of Easter. The word "Lent" comes from an old English word meaning "spring" or "lengthening of the day." These days lead up to the spiritual springtime of new life at Easter.

Lent begins on Ash Wednesday and ends before the Mass of the Lord's Supper on Holy Thursday. Those preparing for sacramental initiation (Baptism, Confirmation, and Eucharist) at Easter enter an intense preparation time during Lent. The rest of us join them in prayerful support. We also prepare to renew our own Baptism at Easter. How do we do this?

During Lent we set out on spiritual journey to follow our baptismal call in a deeper, more intense way. We strengthen ourselves for the journey by prayer, fasting, and almsgiving so that we can bear our "share of hardship for the gospel" as Paul tells Timothy (2 Timothy 1:8–10). Baptism calls us to a daily "dying" and "rising" with Christ. In Baptism, Christ saves us from the power of death and fills us with his own life, a new life of grace.

The images placed before us in Lent are the waters of Baptism and the cross of Jesus. Both remind us of the mystery of our salvation in our Lord Jesus Christ.

The liturgical color for Lent is purple. This color is used to remind us that Lent is a time of renewal, of conversion, and of transformation in Christ.

A LENTEN PRAYER

Focus on Scripture

Readings: Matthew 25:31–40; Joel 2:12–13

Form two groups. Have each group read one of the above passages from Scripture.

Then take a minute to answer these questions:

Name some thing or some strength you could give to others.

The reading from Joel reminds us to rend our hearts, not our garments. What does that mean to you?

Decide together what petitions you wish to offer in today's prayer. Write them on page 27.

In this prayer service, you will be asked to pray for the people in your parish who are preparing for initiation into the Church. Find out who they are and invite them to your prayer service to let them know that you are praying for them. List their names on page 26.

Enriching Your Celebration

Have each person in your group find a penny or another small coin. Use it to represent the "wealth" you possess.

The wealth you have is probably not financial wealth. But perhaps you are "rich" in athletic skills. You could share your athletic skills with younger children after school. Maybe you are "rich" in artistic or academic skills. How might you share this wealth with others?

Share with the other members of your prayer group the wealth that your coin represents to you, then place all the coins in a jar or basket.

Carry the coins as you go in procession to the place where you will pray. Offer these coins to God our Father as symbols of the things you are ready to share with others during the season of Lent.

A LENTEN PRAYER

Gathering Song

All stand.

Greeting

All make the sign of the cross.

Leader: † In the name of the Father, and of the Son, and of the Holy Spirit.

All: Amen.

Leader: My friends,
during these weeks of Lent,
we gather to pray, fast, and give alms
so that we may be ready to fully celebrate
the death and resurrection of the Lord
this Easter. We walk the journey of faith
with those preparing for Baptism
this Easter.

List the names of people in your parish preparing for initiation this Easter:

Leader: For them and for us, we pray:
Good and gracious God,
may we always turn to you
and receive the gift of your love.
Send us your Spirit
to make us strong in faith
and in your love.
We pray this in the name of Jesus.

All: Amen.

Scripture

All sit.

Reader: A reading from. . . .

The group chooses one of these readings:

- Matthew 25:31–40
- Joel 2:12–13

At the end of the reading:

Reader: The word of the Lord.

All: Thanks be to God.

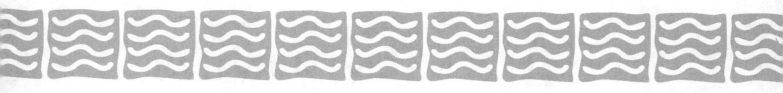

Prayer, Fasting, and Almsgiving

All stand.

Leader: My friends,
let us pray for the Church, the world, and
each other, so that we might always be
mindful of others' needs.

Silent prayer followed by petitions.

*Write your petitions for the Church, the world, and your
community:*

After all the petitions are voiced:

All: We glory in the cross of our Lord Jesus
Christ.

Leader: My friends,
let us also commit ourselves to fasting
during these days, so that this sacrifice
might make us aware of the needs of
others.

*Each person prays silently for God's strength to be faithful
to the commitment to fast for the benefit of others.*

Leader: As we enter our own fast this Lent, let us
remember each other and support each other.

All: We glory in the cross of our Lord Jesus Christ.

Leader: My friends,
let us also commit ourselves to helping
those in need, especially the poor in our
community, through our offering of
money and assistance.

*Each person prays silently for God's strength to be faithful
to the commitment to help the poor. The coins are placed on
the prayer table.*

Leader: As we give from our abundance to those
truly in need, let us remember to pray for
one another and to encourage one
another.

All: We glory in the cross of our Lord Jesus Christ.

Leader: Let us pray the prayer Jesus gave us.

All: Our Father. . . .

Closing Prayer

Leader: Loving God,
help us to do your will
and keep us faithful to you.
We pray this in the name of Jesus.

All: Amen.

Leader: Let us bless the Lord.

All: And give God thanks!

Closing Song

A LENTEN SIGNING WITH THE CROSS

 ## Focus on Scripture
Reading: Psalm 33:12, 20–22

Jesus died so that we might enjoy eternal life with God. His cross is the sign of our salvation and redemption.

In order to be his disciples, Jesus said that we must "take up" our cross and follow him. What is the cross you are being asked to take up this Lent? Ask Jesus to help you to bear it and to follow him.

The cross I "take up" this Lent is:

On page 30 write the intentions for which you as a group wish to pray during this prayer celebration.

Enriching Your Celebration

Using two twigs and a piece of string (about ten inches long), make your own cross.

Hold your cross during the prayer service. Let it serve as a symbol and reminder of your intention to follow Jesus.

A LENTEN SIGNING WITH THE CROSS

Gathering Song

All stand.

Greeting

All make the sign of the cross.

Leader: † In the name of the Father, and of the Son, and of the Holy Spirit.

All: Amen.

Leader: My friends,
let us pray during this season of Lent that God will continue to make us more like him.
We pray this in the name of Jesus.

All: Amen.

Scripture

All sit. Form two groups for the reading of Psalm 33:12, 20–22.

Group 1: Happy the nation whose God is the LORD,
the people chosen as his very own.

Group 2: Our soul waits for the LORD,
who is our help and shield.

Group 1: For in God our hearts rejoice;
in your holy name we trust.

Group 2: May your kindness, LORD, be upon us;
we have put our hope in you.

All: Glory to the Father, and to the Son,
and to the Holy Spirit.
As it was in the beginning, is now,
and will be for ever. Amen.

Signing with the Cross

Stand and turn to face the person next to you.

Leader: My friends,
at Baptism we were signed with the cross of Jesus. God claimed us as his children. Let us pray that we will always remember how much God loves us.

Silent prayer.

As each prayer is made, place your cross in blessing on your neighbor. Place it on each part of the body named in the prayer. Take the time to do this slowly and reverently.

Leader: Receive the sign of the cross on your *forehead,* that you will always remember God's ways.

All: We are all children of God!

Leader: Receive the sign of the cross on your *ears,* that you will always hear the voice of God.

All: We are all children of God!

Leader: Receive the sign of the cross on your *eyes,* that you may always see the world as God sees it.

All: We are all children of God!

Leader: Receive the sign of the cross on your *mouth,* that you will always speak God's care and love.

All: We are all children of God!

Leader: Receive the sign of the cross on your *shoulders,* that you will always find strength in God.

All: We are all children of God!

Leader: Receive the sign of the cross on your *hands,* that you will always reach out to others with Christ's love.

All: We are all children of God!

Leader: Receive the sign of the cross on your *feet,* that you will always follow Jesus.

All: We are all children of God!

Leader: Loving God,
help us to always follow Jesus
and bring his words of love to others.
We pray this in the name of Jesus.

All: Amen.

Prayers of Intercession

Leader: Let us pray for the needs of others.

List your petitions for the needs of the Church, the world, and one another:

All: Lord, hear our prayer.

Leader: Loving God,
we pray for your children throughout
the world.
Help us all to grow in love together.
We ask this in the name of Jesus.

All: Amen.

Leader: Let us pray the prayer Jesus gave us.

All: Our Father. . . .

Closing Prayer

Leader: Loving God,
we continue our Lenten journey
confident of your love for us.
Help us bring that love to all.
We pray this in the name of Jesus.

All: Amen.

Leader: Let us bless the Lord.

All: And give God thanks!

Closing Song

A RECONCILIATION PRAYER SERVICE

 ## Focus on Scripture

Readings: Mark 10:32–34, 42–45; Luke 15:4–7

The reading from Mark reminds us of Christ's mission to serve others and his willingness to sacrifice his life for our salvation. The reading from Luke expresses the joy felt by those who find something or someone who was lost. Choose one reading and read it quietly.

Then take a moment to reflect on these questions. Write a response to the one that applies to the reading you have chosen.

What does it mean to you to be a "servant" to others?

Have you ever felt like the lost sheep who has broken away from the shepherd and the flock?

Enriching Your Celebration

If you feel that there is a difference between the person you'd like to be and the person your actions show you to be, ask God the Father to help you to become more like his Son.

During the prayer service you will have time for silent reflection. Think of something that you wish to ask of God. If you would like to write that petition down, please do so. If you would rather not write it down, keep it to yourself. When we come to the point in the prayer service for silent reflection, speak your petition in your heart.

My petition:

A RECONCILIATION PRAYER SERVICE

This prayer service can be used to prepare for the parish celebration of Reconciliation.

Gathering Song

All stand.

Greeting

All make the sign of the cross.

Leader: † In the name of the Father, and of the Son, and of the Holy Spirit.

All: Amen.

Leader: Dear friends,
let us pray together
that we will be united with Jesus
and share his gift of new life
with all people.
Let us kneel.

Silent prayer.

Leader: Let us stand.
Good and gracious God,
through the death and
resurrection of Jesus,
you give us new life.
Through our practice of penance,
may we be one with Jesus.
We pray this in the name of your Son,
    Jesus Christ.

All: Amen.

Scripture

All sit.

Reader: A reading from. . . .

The group chooses one of these readings:

■ Mark 10:32–34, 42–45   ■ Luke 15:4–7

At the end of the reading:

Reader: The word of the Lord.

All: Thanks be to God.

Examination of Conscience

Remain seated.

Leader: The season of Lent
reminds us to look in our hearts
and see if we have been truly
faithful in our relationship with
God and others.

Reader 1: The Lord says: "You shall love the
Lord your God with your whole heart."
Think about times when you have
shown love for God and times when
you have not.

Silent reflection.

■ *How important is God's love to me?*

■ *How do I show my love to God?*

■ *When I don't show love to God, what are the reasons?*

■ *What do I need from God to help me love God with my whole heart?*

All: Help us, God, to be sorry for our sins.
Give us strength to turn to you.

Reader 2: The Lord says: "Love one another
as I have loved you."
Think about times when you have
shown love to your family,
neighbors, and others, and times when
you have not.

Silent reflection.

■ *Do I treat others as Jesus treats them?*

■ *How do I show my love to others?*

■ *When I don't show love to others, what are the reasons?*

■ *What do I need from God to help me love other people as Jesus loves them?*

All: Help us, God, to be sorry for our sins.
Give us strength to turn to you.

Reader 3: The Lord says: "Be perfect as
your Father is perfect."
Think about times when you have used
your gifts and talents from God to
help others, and times when you have not.

Silent reflection.

■ *Do I take care of myself and develop the gifts God has given me?*

■ *Do I share my talents and gifts to help others?*

■ *When I don't use my talents and gifts to help others, what are the reasons?*

■ *What do I need from God to help me love myself more and share my talents and gifts with others?*

All: Help us, God, to be sorry for our sins.
Give us strength to turn to you.

Act of Repentance

All stand.

Leader: Jesus came to call sinners to God.
Let us acknowledge the sorrow
in our hearts
and promise to try to avoid sin
in the future.

All: I confess to almighty God,
and to you, my brothers and sisters,
that I have sinned through my own fault
in my thoughts and in my words,
in what I have done,
and in what I have failed to do;
and I ask blessed Mary, ever virgin,
all the angels and saints,
and you, my brothers and sisters,
to pray for me to the Lord our God.

Leader: Good and gracious God,
you know all things.
You know that we want to love you.
You know that we want to love others
as Jesus loves them.
You know that we want to use
our gifts and talents to help others.
Look on us with your love and hear us.
We ask this in the name of Jesus.

All: Amen.

Litany

All: God of mercy, hear our prayer.

Reader 1: Give us your strength so we turn from sin.

All: God of mercy, hear our prayer.

Reader 2: Help us to be sorry for our sins.

All: God of mercy, hear our prayer.

Reader 3: Help us to be faithful to you.

All: God of mercy, hear our prayer.

Leader: Let us pray the prayer Jesus gave us.

All: Our Father. . . .

Leader: Let us bless the Lord.

All: And give God thanks!

Closing Song

Celebrating the Easter Triduum and the Easter Season

There are moments, experiences, and events in our lives that are so significant that a single day is not enough to hold them. Moments of great joy or great sorrow take more than a day or a year or sometimes even a lifetime to understand fully. So it is with the death and resurrection of Jesus.

When the spiritual preparation of Lent comes to an end, a new liturgical "day" begins, the Easter Triduum. It begins with the evening Mass of the Lord's Supper on Holy Thursday, sinks into the grief and darkness of the death on Good Friday, emerges into the light and hope of the Easter Vigil, and closes peacefully with evening prayer on Easter Sunday. Still this is not enough time to express the mystery of our redemption and salvation. The Church continues to praise and thank God for fifty *more* days—until Pentecost.

During these great fifty days we struggle, as the disciples did, with our hopes and beliefs, our doubts and confusions. With the disciples at Emmaus we may sometimes feel that we journey alone, only to discover that the risen Christ is with us on the way. We stand with Peter, Mary, and John at the empty tomb, gradually understanding that through Christ we, too, have been raised up from sin and death. We share the Eucharist together with the risen Lord and joyfully witness to his presence among us. Truly, even the great fifty days is not enough—we need a lifetime to understand, and an eternity to celebrate, what God has done for us in Jesus Christ.

The liturgical color of the Easter season is white. This color expresses our joy and peace in the risen Lord and in the new life he has won for us.

THE EASTER TRIDUUM

 ## Focus on Scripture

Readings for:

- **Holy Thursday:** 1 Corinthians 11:23–26
- **Good Friday:** 1 Peter 2:21–24
- **The Easter Vigil:** Philippians 2:5–11
- **Easter Sunday:** Acts 10:40–43

To prepare for your prayer service, read the Scripture passage for the day to yourself. Write down one phrase from the reading that you think is really important. Share the phrase you chose with your family or your group before you begin the celebration.

Holy Thursday:

Good Friday:

Easter Vigil:

Easter Sunday:

Enriching Your Celebration

For each day of the celebration, prepare a different symbol to represent the various aspects of Christ's paschal mystery. As you make your response after the opening prayer, hold up the symbol for that day.

For Holy Thursday: a cup, symbolizing our continual willingness to proclaim Christ's death through our participation in the celebration of the Eucharist.

For Good Friday: a rock, which withstands exposure to all the elements, symbolizing Christ's willingness to endure all things, even death on the cross, for us.

For the Easter Vigil: a large white candle, to symbolize Christ's victory over death, bringing light to the world.

For Easter Sunday: a lily, to symbolize the new life which is ours through the resurrection of our Lord Jesus Christ.

THE EASTER TRIDUUM

This prayer service can be celebrated at home.

Greeting

All make the sign of the cross.

Leader: † In the name of the Father, and of the Son, and of the Holy Spirit.

All: Amen.

Leader: Dear family [and friends],
we come together in prayer
on these most holy days
to remember God's love
given to us in Jesus,
and to share in that love today.

We have a different response for each day of the Triduum.

On Holy Thursday Evening the response is:

All: Jesus is food for the world!

On Good Friday the response is:

All: Jesus is freedom for the world!

For the Easter Vigil (Saturday) the response is:

All: Jesus is life for the world!

On Easter Sunday the response is:

All: Jesus Christ is risen, Alleluia!

Scripture

All sit.

Reader: A reading from. . . .

- Holy Thursday: 1 Corinthians 11:23–26

- Good Friday: 1 Peter 2:21–24

- Holy Saturday: Philippians 2:5–11

- Easter Sunday: Acts 10:40–43

At the end of the reading:

Reader: The word of the Lord.

All: Thanks be to God.

Keeping Vigil

Leader: During these holy days,
we are mindful of God's call
to each of us to follow Jesus.
Let us pray for God's strength
and guidance.

On Holy Thursday:

Leader: That, like Jesus, we will serve the needs of others.

All: Jesus is food for the world!

List some ways you can serve the needs of others:

On Good Friday:

Leader: That, like Jesus, we trust God's will for us.

All: Jesus is freedom for the world!

List ways you can respond to God's call to you to love and care for others:

For the Easter Vigil (Saturday):

Leader: That, like Jesus, we will bring healing to others.

All: Jesus is life for the world!

List some ways you can bring healing to others:

On Easter Sunday:

Leader: That, like Jesus, we will share with others God's promise of a new life of peace.

All: Jesus Christ is risen, alleluia!

List some ways you can bring Jesus to others:

Leader: Let us pray the prayer Jesus gave us.

All: Our Father. . . .

Exchange of Peace

Leader: Dear family [and friends],
as a sign of our unity in Jesus,
let us offer each other a sign of peace.

All exchange the sign of peace.

Closing Prayer

Leader: Loving God,
as we journey together in faith,
help us to better understand
how we can be faithful followers
of Jesus.
We ask this in Jesus' name.

All: Amen.

Leader: Let us bless the Lord.

All: And give God thanks!

An Easter Prayer

 ## Focus on Scripture

Readings: Acts 13:30–33; 1 Peter 2:9–10; Romans 6:8–11

Form three groups. Each group reads one of the Scripture passages that is suggested for the prayer service.

Each group acts as a different television news service. Each news program must inform its audience about the information it has just received from the reading. (None of you has ever read this information before.)

Group 1 reads Acts 13:30–33. You are being asked to explain to everyone else what the "good news" is that Paul preached (and that Luke recorded in the Acts of the Apostles).

Group 2 reads from 1 Peter 2:9–10. This group must find out how God has changed life for the community. (Tell/show us what life was like before Christ and then after Christ became a part of the community.)

Group 3, after reading Romans 6:8–11, must explain to the other two groups why the apostle Paul believes people can live forever.

Now as a group, choose the reading you wish to use in the prayer. Then plan the prayers of intercession you wish to make during the prayer service. Write your choices on page 41.

Enriching Your Celebration

All these readings call for our proclamation of Christ's resurrection. If anyone in your group has a trumpet, horn, or flute, use it during the prayer service.

When you blow into a horn, you call people to attention. When you reply, "Alleluia, alleluia, alleluia" during the Easter Proclamation, use the horn to call out to God and everyone else that you are ready to proclaim the good news of the gospel to all who are willing to listen.

AN EASTER PRAYER

We celebrate the risen Christ among us! If possible, gather around the Easter candle for this celebration.

Gathering Song

All stand.

Greeting

Someone is assigned to light the Easter candle.

All make the sign of the cross.

Leader: † Light and peace in Jesus Christ, our risen Lord!

All: Thanks be to God!

Leader: My friends, let us rejoice with all creation: Our Lord Jesus Christ is risen!

All: Alleluia, alleluia, alleluia! *(sung acclamation)*

Easter Proclamation

Remain standing. Form two groups.

Group 1: To the Paschal Victim let us sing our praise.

All: Alleluia, alleluia, alleluia!

Group 2: The Lamb has redeemed us. The risen Christ reconciles us to the Father.

All: Alleluia, alleluia, alleluia!

Group 1: Death and life were locked in struggle. But now Christ is the Prince of Life, never more to die.

All: Alleluia, alleluia, alleluia!

Group 2: Tell us, Mary, what did you see? "I saw the tomb of the now living Christ."

All: Alleluia, alleluia, alleluia!

Group 1: "I saw the angels who gave witness; and the cloths that had covered him."

All: Alleluia, alleluia, alleluia!

Group 2: "Christ, my hope, is risen. He goes before us to Galilee."

All: Alleluia, alleluia, alleluia!

All: We know that Christ is risen from the dead. Have mercy on us, risen Lord!

Scripture

All sit during the reading of Scripture.

Reader: A reading from. . . .

The group chooses one of these readings:

- Acts 13:30–33
- Romans 6:8–11
- 1 Peter 2:9–10

At the end of the reading:

Reader: The word of the Lord.

All: Thanks be to God.

Prayers of Intercession

Leader: My friends,
with hearts filled with joy,
we turn to God
with the needs of the Church, the world,
and one another.

*Direct your petitions for the Church, the world, your
community and your own special needs to the risen Lord.*

Leader: Loving God,
filled with Easter joy,
we confidently place these prayers
in your hands.
We pray this in the name of Jesus.

All: Amen.

Leader: Let us pray the prayer Jesus gave us.

All: Our Father. . . .

Exchange of Peace

Leader: Dear friends,
        as a sign of our unity in the risen
          Christ,
        let us offer each other a sign
          of peace.

All exchange the sign of peace.

Closing Prayer

Leader: Loving God,
        we thank you for this Easter feast.
        May the Risen One always live
          in our hearts.

All: Amen.

Closing Song

A Celebration of Our Initiation

Focus on Scripture
Reading: Galatians 3:26–27 and 4:6

Quietly read from page 44 the excerpt from Paul's letter to the Galatians. Isn't it amazing? We are God's children. Through Christ we are united to him and to one another in a bond of love. The spirit of Christ is in us, praying to the Father.

What does it mean to you to be "clothed" with Christ?

Take a few minutes now to choose the intercessions the group would like to make in this prayer. Write your choices on page 45.

Enriching Your Celebration

The Easter candle is the symbol of the light of Christ risen in glory who enlightens the darkness of our hearts and minds. This celebration takes place around the Easter candle or, if that is not possible, around another candle that represents it. Each person carries an individual candle that will be lit from the Easter candle during the prayer. A bowl of holy water, a reminder of the waters of Baptism, may be placed on the table along with a Bible from which we will hear God's word.

(Note: If fire laws do not permit lit candles in schools, use battery-operated ones.)

A CELEBRATION OF OUR INITIATION

A bowl of holy water and a Bible should be placed on a nearby table. If the celebration is not held around the Easter candle, another candle representing the Easter candle should be on the table. Each person in the group holds an unlit taper.

Gathering Song

Greeting

A volunteer lights the Easter candle.

All make the sign of the cross.

Leader: † Light and peace in Jesus Christ, our risen Lord!

All: Thanks be to God!

Leader: Let us rejoice with all creation: Our Lord Jesus Christ is risen!

All: Alleluia, alleluia, alleluia!
(sung acclamation)

Scripture

All sit during the reading of Scripture.

Reader: A reading from the letter of Paul to the Galatians.
(Galatians 3:26–27; 4:6)

For through faith you are all
  children of God in Christ Jesus.
For all of you who were baptized
  into Christ have clothed
    yourselves with Christ. . . .
As proof that you are children,
  God sent the spirit of his Son
    into our hearts,
crying out, "Abba, Father!"

At the end of the reading:

Reader: The word of the Lord.

All: Thanks be to God.

Reflection on Baptism

All stand.

Leader: Let us pray for a deeper understanding of the mystery of our Baptism.

This Eastertime
the Church celebrates
the sacrament of Baptism
in which God has washed away
our sins in water
and given us new life in the Spirit.
Through faith and Baptism
we are indeed a new people,
a new creation.
May we who have been
enlightened by Christ
always live as children of light
with the fire of faith alive in our hearts.

All: Amen. Alleluia!

If possible, each one in turn lights his or her taper from the Easter candle.

Leader: The Spirit came upon
the waters of creation.
The waters of the flood
ended with a sign of your promise.
The waters of the Red Sea
opened to lead the people to freedom.
Jesus was baptized by John
in the waters of the Jordan.
We were baptized into the
waters of new life.

And so we proclaim our faith:
Do you believe in God, the Father?

All: I do believe!

Leader: Do you believe in Jesus, the Christ?

All: I do believe!

Leader: Do you believe in the Holy Spirit?

All: I do believe!

Extinguish the candles and gather in a circle. The leader uses the holy water to bless one person from the group by tracing the sign of the cross with water on the forehead. That person then blesses the next in the same way. The last person blesses the leader.

Leader: Through the waters of Baptism, we are born anew and are children of God.

All: Alleluia, alleluia, alleluia!

Leader: We who are born again with water and the Holy Spirit place our hope in the kingdom of heaven. And so we offer our prayers for the Church and for the world.

Offer your prayers of intercession for the Church, the world, your community, yourselves.

Closing Prayer

Leader: It is good to give thanks to God! In gratitude for the sacrament of Baptism, let us pray as Jesus taught us.

Form two groups to pray the Our Father:

Group 1: Our Father, who art in heaven,

Group 2: hallowed be thy name;

Group 1: thy kingdom come;

Group 2: thy will be done on earth as it is in heaven.

Group 1: Give us this day our daily bread;

Group 2: and forgive us our trespasses

Group 1: as we forgive those who trespass against us;

Group 2: and lead us not into temptation,

Group 1: but deliver us from evil.

All: Amen.

Leader: Go in peace.

All: Thanks be to God!

Closing Song

A Prayer Celebration for Pentecost

 ## Focus on Scripture

Readings: John 20:19–23; Acts 2:1–4; Ephesians 4:1–6

The Holy Spirit came upon Jesus' disciples at Pentecost, fifty days after his resurrection, filling them with spiritual gifts. We are sealed with the Spirit in the sacrament of Confirmation and are, in turn, filled with the same spiritual gifts. The readings for this prayer service name these gifts. They are wisdom, understanding, right judgment, courage, knowledge, reverence, and wonder and awe. The gifts of the Spirit empower us to live as Christ's followers with conviction and joy and to make a difference in our world.

Which gift of the Spirit do you need to develop more fully in your life?

Choose the Scripture reading you wish to use in the prayer service.

Enriching Your Celebration

Each one in the group cuts out a paper flame. On the flame each one writes the name of the gift of the Holy Spirit he or she intends to use for the good of others during the weeks of Ordinary Time.

All the flames are then attached to a piece of yarn or ribbon and hung in a place where the air will gently move them during the prayer as a reminder of the presence of the Holy Spirit among us.

A PRAYER CELEBRATION FOR PENTECOST

If possible, gather around the Easter candle in your parish church for this prayer.

Gathering Song

All stand.

Greeting

Someone is assigned to light the Easter candle.

All make the sign of the cross.

Leader: † Light and peace in Jesus Christ,
our risen Lord!

All: Thanks be to God!

Leader: My friends,
let us rejoice with all creation:
Jesus Christ, our Lord, is risen!

All: Alleluia, alleluia, alleluia!

Pentecost Proclamation

Remain standing. Form two groups.

Group 1: Come, Holy Spirit,
shine your light on us.
Come, Father of the poor.
Come, giver of God's gifts.

All: Come, Holy Spirit, come.

Group 2: Kindly Paraclete,
you bring to our souls
your comfort and compassion.

All: Come, Holy Spirit, come.

Group 1: You lighten our heavy hearts,
you strengthen us in temptation,
and you comfort us in sorrow.

All: Come, Holy Spirit, come.

Group 2: Light most blessed,
shine on our hearts!
For without you,
we can do nothing!

All: Come, Holy Spirit, come.

Group 1: With your grace
wash us clean from sin,
bring us your healing,
change our hardened hearts,
and guide us on our way.

All: Come, Holy Spirit, come.

Group 2: Renew us with
your gifts of grace;
help us to walk in holiness now
so that we may live forever with God.

All: Come, Holy Spirit, come.

Scripture

All sit during the reading of Scripture.

Reader: A reading from. . . .

The group chooses one of these readings:

■ John 20:19–23   ■ Acts 2:1–4

■ Ephesians 4:1–6

At the end of the reading:

Reader: The word of the Lord.

All: Thanks be to God.

Reflection on the Gifts of the Spirit

Leader: The Lord Jesus
promised to send us the gift of the
Spirit
to be our helper and guide.

Reader 1: The Spirit gifts us with wisdom.

Reader 2: The Spirit gifts us with
understanding.

Reader 3: The Spirit gifts us with right
judgment.

Reader 4: The Spirit gifts us with courage.

Reader 5: The Spirit gifts us with knowledge.

Reader 6: The Spirit gifts us with reverence.

Reader 7: The Spirit gifts us with the
wonder and awe we feel
in God's presence.

Silent reflection on the gifts of the Spirit.

Come, Holy Spirit

All stand.

Leader: Come, Holy Spirit,
fill the hearts of your faithful.

All: And kindle in them the fire of
your love.

Leader: Send forth your Spirit
and they shall be created.

All: And you will renew the face of the
earth.

Leader: Let us pray.
Good and gracious God,
you send us the gift of the Spirit
to strengthen and renew us.
May we always desire what is good
and holy.
We pray this in the name of Jesus.

All: Amen.

Closing Prayer

Leader: Let us pray as Jesus taught us.

All: Our Father. . . .

Leader: Let us bless the Lord!

All: And give God thanks!

Closing Song

CELEBRATING ORDINARY TIME

The remaining prayer celebrations are to be celebrated during the part of the year called Ordinary Time. Remember: This name does not mean that this is the "uninteresting" season of the liturgical year. The word *ordinary* refers, rather, to "ordinal" or "not seasonal" time. During Ordinary Time, we celebrate the entire life of Christ as it is recorded in order in one of the four gospels.

During the other seasons of the liturgical year, a specific aspect of the mystery of Christ is the focus of our celebrations. But in Ordinary Time, the Church devotes its prayer to all the aspects of the mystery of Christ. Throughout this season we are presented with all of the teachings and miracles of Christ's ministry. And just as his first disciples did, we learn, through his words and works, what it means to be his followers. So you see Ordinary Time is not very ordinary at all!

The prayer celebrations in this section celebrate the beginning and end of the liturgical year; the gratitude we feel for all of God's gifts; the love we feel towards Mary, Mother of God and Jesus' first disciple; and the gift of eternal life which the saints now share and which we believe will be ours as well at the end of our "ordinary" lives.

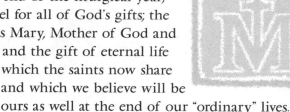

A PRAYER FOR BEGINNINGS AND ENDINGS

Focus on Scripture

Beginnings: When the disciples chose to become friends with Jesus and to follow him, they made a decision based on faith.

 Readings: John 1:35–39 or John 14:5–6

What do you think the disciples found so compelling, so attractive, in Jesus?

Endings: Friendship has many benefits. The readings for this prayer service tell us about the benefits the disciples received through their friendship with Christ.

 Readings: Matthew 28:16–20 or Mark 16:15–20

Do you recognize a benefit that you have received through Christ's friendship? For example: Are you more patient, considerate, or trusting?

Choose the readings you wish for *Beginnings* or *Endings* and then the prayer intentions you wish to offer as a group. Write them on page 52.

Enriching Your Celebration

You buy postcards to remember places or experiences that are important to you. If there were a postcard to remind you of this liturgical year, what would it look like? Do your best to sketch that postcard. Post your cards in the place where you will meet for this prayer.

BEGINNINGS AND ENDINGS

This celebration can be used at both the beginning and ending of the "ordinary" year.

Gathering Song

All stand.

Beginnings:

or

Endings:

Greeting

Leader: † In the name of the Father, and of the Son, and of the Holy Spirit.

All: Thanks be to God!

Leader: Rejoice in the Lord always!

All: It is good to give praise to God!

Scripture

All sit during the reading of Scripture.

Reader: A reading from. . . .

The group chooses one of these readings:

Beginnings:
- John 1:35–39
- John 14:5–6

Endings:
- Matthew 28:16–20
- Mark 16:15–20

At the end of the reading:

Reader: The word of the Lord.

All: Thanks be to God.

Shared Reflection

The group takes time to reflect prayerfully on these or similar questions.

Beginnings
- *What do I hope to learn this year?*
- *How can I follow Jesus today?*
- *How can I help others know about Jesus?*

Endings
- *What is one new thing I learned about my life with God?*
- *How can I bring the good news of Jesus to others?*
- *How do I keep God's love alive all year?*

Group Recognition and Affirmation

All stand.

Leader: Dear friends,
we are called and chosen by God
to live in friendship and love.
As we [begin/end] this year together,
let us recognize the presence of God
in each other and give thanks.

The leader goes to each person in the group individually and says:

Leader: [Name], you are a child of God!

All: *Beginnings:* Learn to know and love God!
Endings: Always walk in God's light!

All: *After all in the group have been named:*
We thank you, God, for one another!

Prayer of Praise

Form two groups. All open hands in a gesture of prayerful praise.

All: We praise you, we bless you forevermore!

Group 1: You are God: we praise you;
you are the Lord: we acclaim you;
you are the eternal Father:
all creation worships you.

All: We praise you, we bless you forevermore!

Group 2: To you all the angels sing in praise:
Holy, holy, holy Lord,
God of power and might,
heaven and earth are full of your glory.

All: We praise you, we bless you forevermore!

Group 1: The apostles praise you.
The prophets and martyrs praise you.
The Church praises you.

All: We praise you, we bless you forevermore!

Group 2: God the Father, we praise you.
Christ, the Son, we praise you.
Holy Spirit, we praise you.

All: We praise you, we bless you forevermore!

Prayers of Intercession

Leader: My friends,
as we [begin/end] this year together,
let us place our cares in God's hands.

Write your own prayers of intercession for the Church, the world, and your community:

Reader: For all of us here as we [begin/end] this time together to learn about God's word,

(Spend a moment in silent prayer for one another.)

we pray to the Lord.

All: Lord, hear our prayer.

Leader: Let us pray the prayer Jesus gave us.

All: Our Father. . . .

Leader: Go in peace.

All: Thanks be to God!

Closing Song

A PRAYER OF THANKSGIVING

Focus on Scripture

Readings: 1 Corinthians 1:3–9; Ephesians 1:3–6

The Scripture readings for this prayer service talk about the blessings we have received from God. Take a moment to read silently one of the Scripture passages. Then choose the reading you wish to use in the prayer service.

During this prayer service, you will be asked to name, as a group, the different gifts for which you are grateful. Before making your group selection, take a minute to recall the blessings God has given you this year and silently thank him for these special gifts. Then together choose those things for which your group is particularly grateful. Name some of the ways you have been blessed by God this year. Write them in the space at the left.

Enriching Your Celebration

Being thankful to God is one of the hallmarks of the Christian. God asks us to show our gratitude by sharing what we have with others.

Well in advance of this prayer celebration form two committees. The first committee will collect food items for those in need. The second committee will collect clothing items for the homeless. The third will be asked to collect books or cards for people in hospitals and nursing homes.

All process to the place of prayer carrying the gifts to be shared. At the part of the prayer service called "Gifts for Those in Need," the collected gifts should be brought to the prayer table.

Afterwards, make sure that your gifts go to those in need. (Your parish outreach program or St. Vincent de Paul Society can help you.)

PREPARATION

A PRAYER OF THANKSGIVING

Gathering Song

All stand.

Greeting

All make the sign of the cross.

Leader: † In the name of the Father, and of the Son, and of the Holy Spirit.

All: Amen.

Leader: All good gifts come to us from God. Today we gather to give thanks to God and to ask his continued blessings on us, our families, and our community.

All: Rejoice in the Lord always!

Litany of Thanksgiving

Leader: Let us give thanks to God.

Reader 1: For the gifts of the earth.

Name the gifts of the earth for which you are grateful:

Reader 2: For the gifts of family.

Name the gifts of family for which you are grateful:

Reader 3: For the gifts of friends.

Name the gifts of friends for which you are grateful:

Reader 4: For the gifts of our community.

Name the gifts of the community for which you are grateful:

Reader 5: For the gifts of the Church.

Name the gifts of the Church for which you are grateful:

Reader 6: For the gifts of love and life with God.

Name the gifts of God's life and love for which you are grateful:

Leader: What else should we give thanks for?

Name other gifts for which you are grateful.

All: We thank you, O God!

Scripture

All sit during the reading of Scripture.

Reader: A reading from. . . .

The group chooses one of these readings:

■ 1 Corinthians 1:3–9   ■ Ephesians 1:3–6

At the end of the reading:

Reader: The word of the Lord.

All: Thanks be to God.

Gifts for Those In Need

Representatives bring the gifts of the group to the prayer table as each group prays.

Leader: God gives us many things
for which we are grateful.
All the gifts from God
are to be shared with others
so no one will be in need.
Let us pray that the Spirit
will give us the strength we need
to freely share with others
all the gifts we have received.

Group 1: I was hungry and you gave me food.
I was thirsty and you gave me drink.

Silent reflection.

All: As long as you did it for the least of my sisters and brothers, you did it for me.

Group 2: I was a stranger and you welcomed me.
I was naked and you clothed me.

Silent reflection.

All: As long as you did it for the least of my sisters and brothers, you did it for me.

Group 3: I was ill and you comforted me.
I was in prison and you came to visit me.

Silent reflection.

All: As long as you did it for the least of my sisters and brothers, you did it for me.

Closing Prayer

Leader: Let us pray the prayer Jesus taught us.

All: Our Father. . . .

Leader: Let us bless the Lord!

All: And give God thanks!

Closing Song

A PRAYER TO MARY, MOTHER OF GOD

 ## Focus on Scripture

Reading: Luke 1:46–50, 53–54

Catholics have a special devotion to the Blessed Mother. Why? Mary gave herself completely to God. When the angel Gabriel appeared to tell her that she would bear the Son of God she replied, "May it be done to me according to your word" (Luke 1:38). In all things Mary did God's will, not her own. She is the virgin Mother of Jesus, the Son of God. In her unique role she teaches us how to be a disciple, a true follower of Christ. We are also devoted to Mary because she acts as our great intercessor, who prays to God on our behalf.

The verses from Luke we will read in this prayer service are taken from the Magnificat, Mary's prayer of praise. In these verses, Mary celebrates the greatness of God. Take a few moments to read the Scripture passage to yourself.

Would you like to give thanks to Mary for something she has done? Compose your own verse of thanks.

Share your prayer to Mary with your group.

Enriching Your Celebration

We often place flowers before statues of Mary on her feast days. You might choose to use flowers as symbols of your gratitude towards Our Lady. You may also want to present her with a gift that is representative of the talents of your group. Think about ways you could incorporate your talents into a gift for the Blessed Mother. (You may want to read the story by Anatole France, *Our Lady's Juggler*, for encouragement.)

You might wish to use the verses you wrote in gratitude to Mary to compose a group poem, a rap, or a song.

A PRAYER TO MARY, MOTHER OF GOD

This celebration can be used for any of the feasts that celebrate Mary, Mother of God.

Gathering Song

All stand.

Greeting

All make the sign of the cross.

Leader: † In the name of the Father, and of the Son, and of the Holy Spirit.

All: Amen.

Leader: How good it is for us to come together to remember and celebrate how God has blessed us. God gives us Mary as an example of how we can say yes to God's will.

All: Rejoice in the Lord always!

Scripture

All sit. Form two groups for the reading of the Scripture.

Leader: A reading from the Gospel of Luke. (*Luke 1:46–50, 53–54*)

Group 1: My soul proclaims the greatness of the Lord; my spirit rejoices in God my savior.

Group 2: For he has looked upon his handmaid's lowliness; behold, from now on will all ages call me blessed.

Group 1: The Mighty One has done great things for me, and holy is his name.

Group 2: His mercy is from age to age to those who fear him.

Group 1: The hungry he has filled with good things; the rich he has sent away empty.

Group 2: He has helped Israel his servant, remembering his mercy.

At the end of the reading:

Leader: The word of the Lord.

All: Thanks be to God.

Litany of Our Lady

All stand.

Leader: Let us pray to God in gratitude for the gift of Mary to the Church.

Group 1: God, our Father,
All: have mercy on us.

Group 2: Christ, the Son,
All: have mercy on us.

Group 1: Holy Spirit, Comforter and Guide,
All: have mercy on us.

Group 2: Mary, Mother of God,
All: pray for us.

Group 1: Mary, Mother of the Church,
All: pray for us.

Group 2: Mary, Queen of Heaven,
All: pray for us.

Group 1: Mary, the Immaculate Conception,
All: pray for us.

Group 2: Mary, Our Lady of Guadalupe,
All: pray for us.

Group 1: Mary, Our Lady of Lourdes,
All: pray for us.

Group 2: Mary, Our Lady of Mount Carmel,
All: pray for us.

Group 1: Mary, Our Lady of Sorrows,
All: pray for us.

Group 2: Mary, Our Lady of the Rosary,
All: pray for us.

Silently reflect on the images and titles of Mary.

Prayer to the Blessed Virgin

All: We turn to you for protection,
holy Mother of God.
Listen to our prayers
and help us in our needs.
Save us from every danger,
glorious and blessed Virgin.

Exchange of Peace

Leader: Let us pray the prayer Jesus gave us.

All: Our Father. . . .

Leader: Dear friends,
as a sign of our unity in the Risen Christ,
let us offer each other a sign of peace.

All exchange the sign of peace.

Closing Prayer

Leader: Good and gracious God,
you bless us
with the presence of the Virgin Mary,
Queen of Heaven.
May her prayers lead us to you.
We pray this in the name of Jesus.

All: Amen.

Leader: Let us bless the Lord!

All: And give God thanks!

Closing Song

CELEBRATING ALL SAINTS AND ALL SOULS

 ## Focus on Scripture
Reading: Psalm 121:1–2, 5–8

Before the prayer, take a few minutes to read the verses of Psalm 121 slowly and thoughtfully. Then respond to the question below.

Think of someone you loved who has died. How did this person affect your life?

Think of a story about this person that captures his or her best quality and share that story with your prayer group. If it is too difficult for you to talk about the person who has died, write out the story you would want to share.

Now, together, choose the intentions for which you would particularly like to pray in this celebration. Write them on page 61.

Enriching Your Celebration

With two twigs and about ten inches of yarn or string, make a cross. On a strip of construction paper about five inches long, write down the name of someone you know who has died. If you do not know anyone who has died, write down the name of a saint.

Place the piece of paper diagonally over the point where the two twigs meet. Turn your cross over and tape the two ends of the paper together. The strip of paper with the person's name on it should hang in a ring around your cross.

Carry the cross you made into the place where you will pray and hold it during the prayer service.

CELEBRATING ALL SAINTS

This celebration can also be used when there is a death in the parish community.

Gathering Song

All stand.

Greeting

All make the sign of the cross.

Leader: † In the name of the Father, and of the Son, and of the Holy Spirit.

All: Amen.

Leader: Holy is God! Holy, Immortal One!

All: We praise you, O God!

Leader: We gather today to honor all the unnamed saints, the holy women and men whose heroic lives are an example to us. We also remember those who have died in our parish and in our families. We pray for them and for each other.

Scripture

All sit. Form two groups for the reading of Psalm 121:1–2, 5–8.

Group 1: I raise my eyes toward the mountains.
From where will my help come?
My help comes from the LORD,
the maker of heaven and earth.

Group 2: The LORD is your guardian;
the LORD is your shade
at your right hand.
By day the sun cannot harm you,
nor the moon by night.

Group 1: The LORD will guard you from all evil,
will always guard your life.
The LORD will guard your coming
and going
both now and forever.

All bow during the doxology.

Group 2: Glory to the Father, and to the Son,
and to the Holy Spirit.
As it was in the beginning, is now,
and will be for ever. Amen.

Litany of the Saints

All stand.

Leader: Lord, have mercy.

All: Lord, have mercy.

Leader: Christ, have mercy.

All: Christ, have mercy.

Leader: Lord, have mercy.

All: Lord, have mercy.

After each saint's name, all pray: "Pray for us."

Leader: Holy Mary, Mother of God. . . .
Saint John the Baptist. . . .
Saint Thomas. . . .
Saint Francis. . . .
Saint Rose of Lima. . . .
Saint Ignatius Loyola. . . .
Saint Frances Xavier Cabrini. . . .
Saint Elizabeth Ann Seton. . . .
Saint Andrew Kim of Korea. . . .
Saint Catherine. . . .

Add names of other saints that are important to you and your parish:

AND ALL SOULS

Litany of Remembrance

All sit.

Leader: Let us remember those who have died.

Read the name of the person written on your cross.

All: We praise you, O God,
for the lives of those we love!

Leader: Eternal rest grant unto them, O Lord,

All: And let perpetual light shine upon them.

Leader: May they rest in peace.

All: Amen.

Leader: May their souls and the souls
of all the faithful departed,
through the mercy of God,
rest in peace.

All: Amen.

Prayers of Intercession

All stand.

Leader: My friends, let us place our cares
in God's hands.

Write your prayers of intercession for the Church, the world, and your community:

All: Lord, hear our prayer.

Leader: Let us pray the prayer Jesus gave us.

All: Our Father. . . .

Closing Prayer

Leader: Good and gracious God, we honor the
memory of those who have died.
May they, along with the saints,
share the fullness of your love and life.
We pray this in the name of Jesus.

All: Amen.

Leader: Let us bless the Lord!

All: And give God thanks!

Closing Song

PLANNING A PRAYER CELEBRATION FOR _____

On these two pages you have the opportunity to plan your own prayer celebration. Work together on each section. When you have finished, you will be ready to pray together.

Choosing a Focus

The liturgical year is rich in possibilities for prayer. A focus might be: gratitude, friendship, discipleship, loss, trust, justice, or . . . ?

Our theme: _____

Enriching the Theme

In what ways can your theme be expressed in words or actions?

Our symbol: _____

How it will be used: _____

Songs or Hymns

Songs or hymns are prayers. A great saint once said that the one "who sings prays twice." What songs suit your theme? Do you need a tape or a CD to support the music?

Opening song: _____

Closing song: _____

Opening Prayer

This prayer calls the group together and helps you to focus on the purpose of your celebration. The sacramentary or the *Book of Blessings* may help you find the right words.

_____

_____

_____

_____

Readings

All the readings the Church uses during the liturgical year can be found in the lectionary. A good place to look for readings when selecting a special theme is in the section called "Masses for Various Occasions." If you choose a psalm, you might want to have it read by two groups, alternating verses.

Readings: _____

_____

Psalm: _____

_____

Prayers of Intercession

Your group should carefully choose the intentions for which you wish to pray. Use the format that is suggested in the other celebrations in this book. Choose the response you wish the group to make.

_____

_____

_____

Response: _____

Materials

Are there any things that need to be provided? For example: Bibles, prayer table, copies of the prayer celebration, symbols, words of songs, musical accompaniment?

_____

_____

_____

_____

Acknowledgments

Scripture selections are taken from the *New American Bible with Revised New Testament and Revised Psalms* Copyright © 1991, 1986, 1970 by the Confraternity of Christian Doctrine, Washington, D.C. Used with permission of copyright owner. All rights reserved. No portion of the *New American Bible* may be reproduced or transmitted by any means without permission in writing from the copyright owner.

Excerpts from the English translation of *The Roman Missal* © 1973, International Committee on English in the Liturgy, Inc. (ICEL); excerpts from the English translation of the *Rite of Christian Initiation of Adults* © 1986, ICEL. All rights reserved.

The English translation of the Lord's Prayer and the Glory to the Father by the International Consultation on English Texts (ICET).